CCSS **Genre** Expository Text

Essential Question
How do teams work together?

D1562809

Firefighting Heroes

by Kate Sinclair

Introduction

Long ago, people needed fire to survive. They used fire to cook and to keep warm, but accidental fire was always a danger. Many buildings were made of wood. The buildings were often surrounded by forest. There was no running water to put out fires. There were no fire departments to call. A fire could destroy an entire village in just moments!

The Great Fire of London destroyed more than 13,000 houses and hundreds of other buildings in the city.

In 1666, a fire—now known as the Great Fire of London—raged in the streets of London for over three days. Thousands of houses were destroyed. Many people died.

The fire started in one small shop. It was a windy day. The wind helped to push the fire quickly across the city. The fire caused a great deal of damage.

People realized that they would have to work together to protect themselves from fire.

CHAPTER 1

United We Stand

Fire was a problem for the first settlers in America. People arrived in Jamestown, Virginia, from England in 1607. In 1608, a fire nearly destroyed the **colony**. Almost all of the houses were burned to the ground.

It was not only Jamestown that suffered harmful fires in the 1600s. There were two big fires in Boston in 1653 and 1676.

People realized that they needed to respond quickly to fires. The **colonists** began to form **volunteer** firefighting teams. Their purpose was to fight fires and to prevent fires from starting.

Fighting Fire in the 1600s

- Buckets of water were kept outside each house at night.
- Volunteers used long poles to collect the buckets.
- Volunteers raced to the fire with the buckets of water.
- Many volunteers were needed.

Fire damaged many buildings in American cities. This building was destroyed in 1882.

William Penn **founded** the city of Philadelphia in 1682. Penn had witnessed the Great Fire of London. He tried to prevent fires when planning his new city. People were told to clean their chimneys regularly. Many new buildings were built from brick instead of wood.

This is the first fire engine ever built in the United States.

Benjamin Franklin was one of our founding fathers. He started a volunteer firefighting group in Philadelphia. Franklin had witnessed terrible fires in Boston and knew the dangers of them.

In 1736, Franklin started a fire brigade called The Union Fire Company. It had 30 volunteers. These volunteers were heroes in their community.

Ben Franklin helped set up a volunteer firefighting company in Philadelphia.

Women Firefighters

Women began volunteering in the 1800s. The first known female volunteer was an African American woman, Molly Williams. Molly fought fires in New York wearing a dress and an apron. In Pittsburgh, Marina Betts was known for throwing buckets of water over men who wouldn't help fight fires!

Working as a team was a very important part of being a volunteer firefighter in Ben Franklin's time. It took many people to collect the buckets of water from outside people's homes and carry them to the fire.

To get the water to the fire as quickly as possible, volunteers would form a line and pass buckets of water from one to another down the line.

Today, we have modern equipment to fight fires, so not as many volunteers are needed. The job is just as important, however, and firefighters still need to work together as a team.

Firefighters work to put out a fire in Atlanta, Georgia.

CHAPTER 2

Firefighters at Work

Today, there are more than 30,000 fire departments in the United States. Almost 90 percent of them are either completely or partly run by volunteers. This amounts to more than 800,000 people! All volunteers have a sense of **civic duty**. They want to help the people in their community.

Today's firefighters use modern equipment, including high-pressure hoses, to fight fires.

Firefighters often work with members of other teams, such as paramedics.

Firefighters work in teams. The captain, who's in charge, gives jobs to each firefighter. These jobs can change at a moment's notice. That means all firefighters must learn to drive the fire truck, hook up the hoses, position the ladders, and enter burning buildings safely.

Volunteer firefighters do more than fight fires. They help out during natural disasters, car accidents, and medical emergencies.

Even if there is not a fire, there's still work to be done. The team needs to wash the fire trucks and take care of the other equipment.

Volunteer firefighters need a lot of training. First, they need to learn about fire safety. They usually have to pass a physical test as well. Firefighters have to be able to crawl through small spaces and move heavy ladders. They have to be able to drag a heavy hose for several hundred feet and carry it up and down several flights of stairs. Finally, they have to be able to carry a 180-pound person through a doorway. They practice by using a dummy.

Firefighters must wear protective gear and carry heavy equipment.

All in a Day's Work

Read about this firefighter's day.

The alarm is ringing. A house is on fire. We run to the fire truck and take our seats. Joe is our driver. My job is to control the hose. Anne looks after the ladders. When we get there, we find that the fire is hard to control. We all have our protective clothing and our breathing **apparatus**. We're not sure if everyone is out of the house. First, we help clear the house. An elderly man is last out. He is having trouble breathing. Peter, our first aid officer, gives him

Firefighters work together at a fire.

oxygen and helps him to breathe steadily again. Our new equipment helps make sure the fire is out. We are all exhausted! But everyone is safe, and the fire is contained.

CHAPTER 3
Safety in the Home

People have been aware of the need for fire prevention and fire safety for a long time. One of a firefighter's jobs is to educate, or teach, people about fire safety. Do you know what to do if there is a fire in your home?

Escape!

Think about the layout of your home. Have a family meeting and talk about the best ways to leave the house, especially at night. Choose a place away from the house to meet. Someone needs to be in charge of "counting heads" to check that everyone is out. Call the fire department as soon as you can, but don't stay in the house to do it.

STOP   **DROP**   **ROLL**

If your clothing catches fire, drop to the floor and roll over to put out the flames.

High-Rise Buildings

If you live in a tall building, check where your nearest fire exit is. Make sure you can find your way there in the dark. When you get out of the building, stay out. Tell the fire department if you think anyone is still inside.

Stairs are the safest way out of a high-rise building during a fire.

A working smoke alarm saves lives!

Smoke Alarms

A working smoke alarm can alert you to a fire at any time of the day or night. Make sure your home has smoke alarms on every level and near the bedrooms. Remember to change the batteries every six months.

Conclusion

People have known for a long time that it's a good idea to work together to protect the community from fires. Today, many people's lives are very busy. It can be difficult for them to find time to volunteer for services such as firefighting. Yet the work of volunteer firefighters is as important today as it has ever been.

Firefighters teach people of all ages about fire safety.

Respond to Reading

Summarize

Use details from *Firefighting Heroes* to summarize the text. Your graphic organizer may help you.

Details

↓

Point of View

Text Evidence

1. How do you know that *Firefighting Heroes* is an expository text? Find two examples of information about firefighters in the text. **GENRE**

2. How does the author describe volunteer firefighters? Give two examples. **AUTHOR'S POINT OF VIEW**

3. What do you think *prevent* on page 4 means? What clues in the sentence help you figure out what it means? **SENTENCE CLUES**

4. Write a paragraph describing how the author feels about volunteer firefighters. **WRITE ABOUT READING**

Compare Texts
Read about a woman who gets help from a very unusual source.

A FAVOR REPAID

Sal Fink was the daughter of a famous Mississippi boatman. She was as brave as her father, and just as loud. When she yelled, her voice echoed through the forest.

One day, Sal heard grunting from the hollow of a tree. She saw three sleeping bear cubs. Sal bent to pat them. Patting wild animals is not a good idea, but Sal was careless about her safety.

Sal heard a low rumble behind her. She turned to face a very angry mother bear. The bear was going to attack! Sal was up to the challenge. First, she yelled. That stopped the bear. Then, she wrestled it to the ground.

Sal had the bear at her mercy. She looked at the bear. Then she looked at the cubs. She patted the bear and walked away.

A couple of years later, Sal was chopping down a tree. She didn't notice that the birds had stopped singing. Suddenly, Sal smelled smoke. She looked around. She could see flames and hear the crackle of burning wood. Every way Sal looked, she could see the flames.

Sal knew how fast wildfires could spread. She didn't know which way to go. She yelled loudly, but there was no one to hear. Or so Sal thought!

Suddenly, a bear came crashing out of the trees. The bear had recognized Sal's voice. It feared fire, but it remembered that Sal had spared its life. The bear ran toward Sal. Then it ran back. Sal realized the bear wanted her to follow.

As Sal ran, she could hear trees falling. They came to the river and plunged in. Sal held onto the bear's fur and was towed to the other side.

Sal clambered out and lay gasping, but safe. The bear looked at her and ambled away. From that time on, Sal would often catch a glimpse of black fur, but she never saw the bear again.

Make Connections

How do Sal and the bear work together in *A Favor Repaid*? ESSENTIAL QUESTION

How are *Firefighting Heroes* and *A Favor Repaid* examples of teamwork? TEXT TO TEXT

Glossary

apparatus *(ap-uh-RAT-uhs)* the equipment needed for a particular purpose *(page 11)*

civic duty *(SIV-ik DEW-tee)* the responsibilities of a citizen *(page 8)*

colonists *(KOL-uh-nists)* early settlers *(page 4)*

colony *(KOL-uh-nee)* a place where people first settle in a land that is new to them *(page 4)*

founded *(FOWND-uhd)* started *(page 5)*

volunteer *(vol-uhn-TEER)* a person who offers to do a job for no payment *(page 4)*

Index

Focus on
Social Studies

Purpose To find out about volunteers.

What to Do

Step 1 ▶ Choose an organization that uses volunteers, such as a food bank or an animal shelter.

Step 2 ▶ Find out as much as you can about the organization, such as how it operates and what its goals are.

Step 3 ▶ Find out what volunteers do.

Step 4 ▶ Write a paragraph about what the organization does.

Step 5 ▶ Write a paragraph about what volunteers do.

Conclusion What did you learn about the organization?